WHEN I AM LAID IN EARTH

(Air, "Dido's Lament")
from the opera *Dido and Aeneas*

HENRY PURCELL
arranged by SYLVIA RABINOF

For Two Pianos, Eight Hands

PIANO I

WHEN I AM LAID IN EARTH

(Air, "Dido's Lament")

from the Opera *Dido and Aeneas*

SECONDO

HENRY PURCELL (1659 - 1695)
arr. by *SYLVIA RABINOF*

* ⌐¬ Solo part to be brought out (all other parts to be played as accompaniment.)

WHEN I AM LAID IN EARTH

(Air, "Dido's Lament")

from the Opera *Dido and Aeneas*

PRIMO

HENRY PURCELL (1659 - 1695)
arr. by SYLVIA RABINOF

* Solo part to be brought out (all other parts to be played as accompaniment.)

4

crescendo
mf
dim. and rit.
pp
a tempo
p
mf
rit.
8va
8va
p
a tempo
pp
crescendo
(8va)
f
dim.
ritenuto
pp

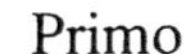

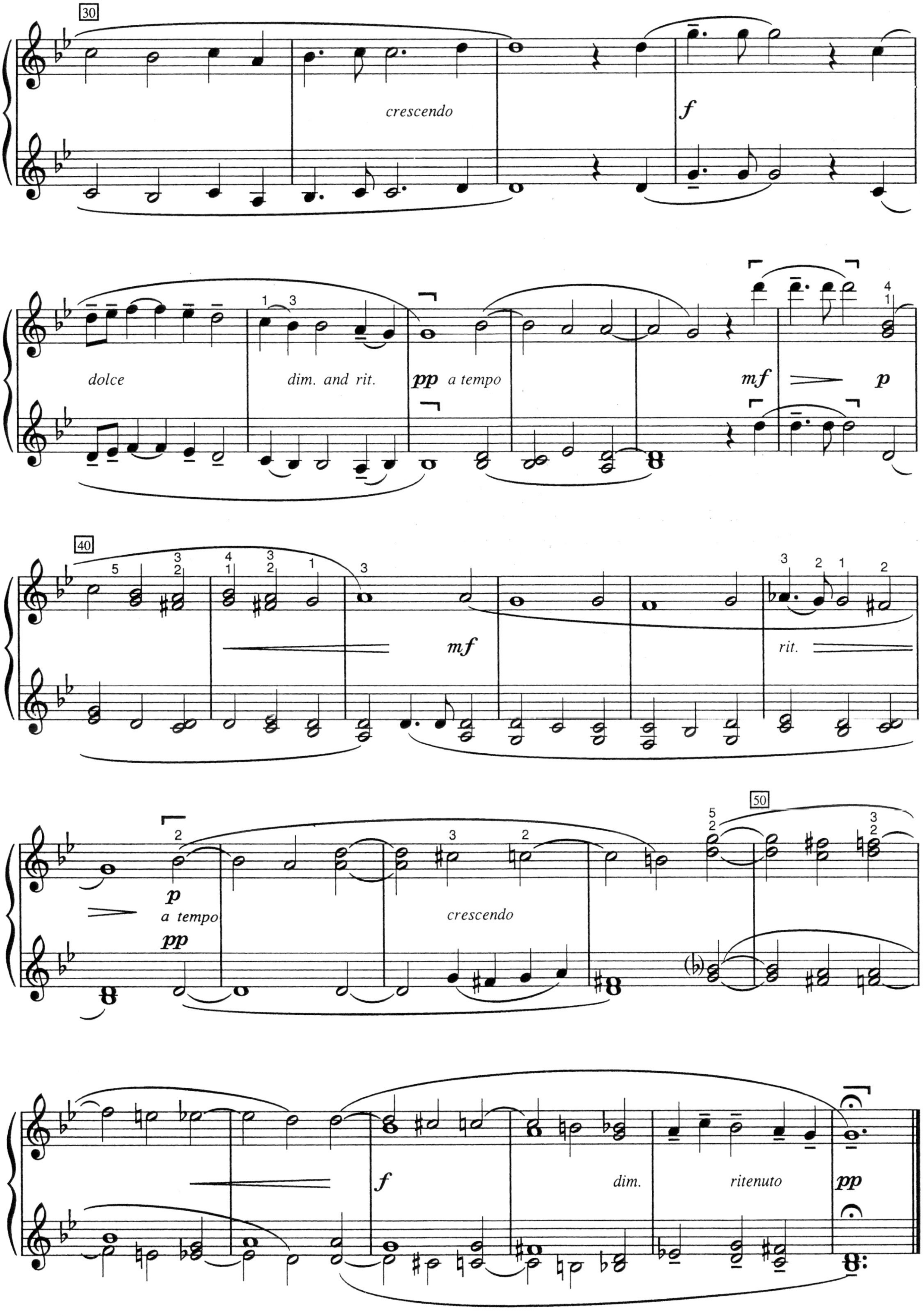
30
crescendo
f
dolce
dim. and rit.
pp a tempo
mf
p
40
mf
rit.
p
a tempo
pp
crescendo
50
f
dim.
ritenuto
pp

WHEN I AM LAID IN EARTH
Air "Dido's Lament" from Dido and Aeneas
by Henry Purcell

Henry Purcell (1659-1695) was known by his contemporaries as the British Orpheus. He was the last of a line of eminent English composers since the pre-Tudor period. His masterpiece, *Dido and Aeneas,* still considered the high point of English opera, was first performed in 1689 "at Mr. Josias Priest's boarding school at Chelsey by young Gentlewomen... to a select audience of their parents and friends." It ends with a poignant, lovely aria "When I Am Laid In Earth" sung by the lovelorn, dying Queen Dido as her hero Aeneas sails away. The orchestral string basses introduce the four-measure ground bass, a chromatic scale moving downward:

which is repeated again and again under the unfolding lament, climaxed by the deeply touching final phrase on high G, with the words:

"Remember me!"

WHEN I AM LAID IN EARTH

(Air, "Dido's Lament")
from the opera *Dido and Aeneas*

HENRY PURCELL
arranged by SYLVIA RABINOF

For Two Pianos, Eight Hands

PIANO II

WHEN I AM LAID IN EARTH

(Air, "Dido's Lament")

from the Opera *Dido and Aeneas*

SECONDO

HENRY PURCELL (1659 - 1695)
arr. by SYLVIA RABINOF

*⌐ ⌐ Solo part to be brought out (all other parts to be played as accompaniment.)

PIANO II

WHEN I AM LAID IN EARTH

(Air, "Dido's Lament")

from the Opera *Dido and Aeneas*

PRIMO

HENRY PURCELL (1659 - 1695)
arr. by SYLVIA RABINOF

*⌐ Solo part to be brought out (all other parts to be played as accompaniment.)

Secondo

30
crescendo
mf
dim. and rit.
pp   a tempo
40
50
rit.
p
a tempo
pp
crescendo
8va
f
dim.
ritenuto
pp
8va
8va

p
crescendo
mf
dim. and rit.
pp
a tempo
mp
p
mf
8va
f expressively
rit.
a tempo
pp
p
crescendo
f
dim. ritenuto
pp

WHEN I AM LAID IN EARTH
Air "Dido's Lament" from Dido and Aeneas
by Henry Purcell

  Henry Purcell (1659-1695) was known by his contemporaries as the British Orpheus. He was the last of a line of eminent English composers since the pre-Tudor period. His masterpiece, *Dido and Aeneas,* still considered the high point of English opera, was first performed in 1689 "at Mr. Josias Priest's boarding school at Chelsey by young Gentlewomen... to a select audience of their parents and friends." It ends with a poignant, lovely aria "When I Am Laid In Earth" sung by the lovelorn, dying Queen Dido as her hero Aeneas sails away. The orchestral string basses introduce the four-measure ground bass, a chromatic scale moving downward:

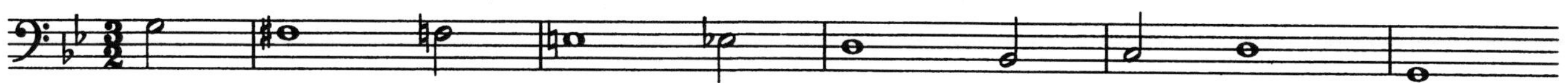

which is repeated again and again under the unfolding lament, climaxed by the deeply touching final phrase on high G, with the words:

"Remember me!"